ALL ABOUT
MOTORCYCLES

Frank Melling

Foulis

Haynes
®

ISBN 0-85429-665-4

A **FOULIS** Motorcycling Book

First published May 1991

Published by
Haynes Publishing Group Ltd
Sparkford, Yeovil, Somerset
BA22 7JJ, England

Haynes Publications Inc
861 Lawrence Drive, Newbury Park, California 91320 USA

British Library Cataloguing in Publication data
Melling, Frank
All about motorcycles.
1. Motorcycles
I. Title
629.2275

ISBN 0-85429-665-4

Library of Congress Catalogue Card Number
90-84484

Editor: Jeff Clew
Cover design: Camway Autographics
Layout design: Tim Rose
Printed in England by J.H. Haynes & Co. Ltd.

Contents

Acknowledgements

A book requiring so much research and technical support cannot be produced without a lot of high quality assistance. It was generously given, in particular from:

Honda (U.K.) Ltd, and especially Bob McMillan and Graham Sanderson. Castrol, through the good offices of Paul Farrell. Cyril Chell of C.G. Chell Motorcycles of Stafford and Alan Dugdale of H. Dugdale Motors, Alvanley, Cheshire.

My thanks also to George Lloyd of G-MAC clothing, Hamilton, Scotland; Renolds Chain; Chris Graham of Britool tools; Nick Jefferies of Allan Jefferies Motorcycles, Saltaire, Yorkshire, and Peter Collins and his Belle Vue Speedway team.

The whole book was produced on Canon word processing equipment supplied and maintained by Kent Office Interiors, of Southport, whose Managing Director, Malcolm Kent, coincidentally happens to be the keenest motorcyclist in Britain.

And finally, my thanks to all those young people who helped in the production of the book by being photographed and interviewed and whose comments were so valuable in improving my early attempts to produce a text which was fun to read as well as being informative. I hope that you all go on to be life-long motorcyclists and have as much fun from bikes as I have.

Frank Melling

4

The First Motorcycles

We are going to begin by looking at the first bikes. They didn't work very well and they were not very fast but they moved without being pedalled or being pulled by a horse and 100 years ago, that was amazing!

When you look at a motorcycle today, have you ever thought what the old bikes were like? Were they easy to ride? How fast did they go? Were they comfortable?

To answer all these questions, we have got to go quite a long way back in time. Not as long as the Romans or even the Normans but back to the Victorian period – about 100 years ago.

Gottlieb Daimler's first motorcycle built in 1885. It wasn't much of a bike but it just about moved without being pedalled. (Photo: EMAP Archives)

5

The world was very different in those days and there must have been a feeling of great excitement. There was a great interest in science and engineering and almost every week, some fantastic new invention appeared. First there were gas lights and then electricity and new cures for many kinds of illnesses were always being announced. Everyone was excited about the future and they were very sure that any problem could be solved. And one of the things which most interested people at this time was how to travel quickly and safely.

Before cars and bikes, the quickest way to get from one part of the world to another was the steam train. And if there wasn't a railway line near to where you wanted to go then the next best thing was a stage coach or paddle steamer. No-one, except the very rich, could get from their own house to where they were going very quickly.

Then, in 1885, a German called Gottlieb Daimler made a small engine which ran off a kind of petrol. It wasn't a very good engine but it just about worked! Daimler fitted the engine into the first motorcycle – except that this one had two little wheels attached to each side in case it fell over, just like an infant's bike.

The following year, another German, Wilhelm Maybach, rode the Daimler bike for a few metres – something which everyone thought was

Many of the roads were covered in sharp stones called flints. These were excellent for horses' hooves but terrible for bike tyres. (Photo: EMAP Archives)

Parbold Hill, the scene of the Liverpool Hill-climbing Competition.

very brave. At last, a way of moving people directly from one place to another had been invented.

Not everybody thought that this was a good idea. In England, there was a law which said that no vehicle powered by an engine could go faster than 4 mph – which is about as fast as you can walk. What was worse was that a man had to march in front of the vehicle waving a red flag to warn citizens of the danger. Even with a 4 mph speed limit **and** a red flag, many people thought that the new motorcycles and cars were dangerous and should be banned.

Although some people were frightened by the new machines, many others thought that they were a very good idea and in 1896, an Act of Parliament was passed which said that there need not be anyone carrying a red flag in front of vehicles and that they could now go at 12 mph – which

was considered to be a fantastic speed then but is still only as fast as you can run.

At the same time, a French engineer called De Dion made the first really good engine for motorcycles and soon everyone was having a try at making complete machines. Many of the first manufacturers were pedal cycle makers and no-one really had any idea how to make a proper motorcycle. Fantastic claims were made for these early machines. E.J. Pennington said his bike could jump rivers when it had difficulty even moving!

Now, everyone knows what a motorcycle looks like but in those early days, no-one understood how to make a proper bike. They didn't know where to put the engine and they didn't know how to make strong frames. Worst of all, they didn't know how to make good brakes so when these first motorcyclists did get going

The first bikes didn't look anything like a modern motorcycle but they got better very soon. If you look carefully, you can see that one rider has fitted gas lights to his bike but he still only has cycle brakes to stop him.
(Photo: EMAP Archives)

In just a few years, the early bike makers had started to produce powerful engines with two, and even four cylinders, which could take their riders all over the country. (Photo: EMAP Archives)

they couldn't stop properly, so they often crashed!

Most of the roads were made of flint chippings – little pieces of stone which made the bike skid and crash when the rider tried to turn a corner. Then there were horseshoe nails to puncture the tyres and horses which were so frightened by the noise that they tried to jump on the bikes and their riders. Life was very exciting for these early motorcyclists!

Yet, despite all these problems the riders grew to love their bikes and became very good at riding them. In 1900, Hubert Egerton rode his Werner motorcycle from Land's End to John O'Groats – which is from one end of Britain to the other. Now, there was no part of the country which could not be reached by these fantastic new machines.

The British Bikes

Today, you won't see many British bikes on the roads but for many years, Britain made the best bikes in the world – and the most! Now, we only make a few. What went wrong?

In 1900, bikes were not very good. They were hard to start, they had poor brakes and not much power but everyone thought they were marvellous! For the first time, a person could have his own individual way of getting about. He had personal transport which he could use the moment he wanted to. Above all else, these first motorcyclists felt the sense of freedom which a bike gave to them.

The same sense of excitement was felt by the motorcycle manufacturers. New designs appeared almost every day. Some were excellent and others silly but each factory learnt from the others and bikes got better and better in just a few years. Then the first World War came in 1914, and the whole world changed. Bikes made in this first period, from 1885 until the end of 1914 are called Veterans and many are still being used today by riders who are re-living how the first motorcyclists rode.

When the war came, the bikes went with the army. The fastest way to carry an urgent message was with a good rider on a bike. Motorcycle and side-

The first bikes used for work instead of pleasure were in the Great War of 1914-1918. In these tough conditions, motorcycles showed that they could do everything that a horse could – and a lot more too! (Photo: EMAP Archives)

9

car outfits transported machine guns very quickly. Because the conditions were so tough, bikes had to become stronger, more powerful and more reliable. Now, the motorcycle wasn't a toy for just a few people but a real working vehicle.

The period after the start of the war, to the end of 1930, is called the Golden Age of British motorcycling. Another name for it is the Vintage period. Some of the most beautiful bikes were made then. Motorcycles made at this time were still being built with the old fashioned craftsmanship of the Edwardians but the designs were new and exciting. There were dozens of motorcycle makers all competing to build faster, safer and more reliable bikes. Gearboxes, which allowed the rider to alter the speed of his bike so that he could go fast on the open roads or slow in towns, were fitted to all bikes and machines had chains to drive the rear wheel instead of the leather belts which the first bikes used. No-one missed the end of the leather belts which broke when the weather was dry and slipped when it was wet!

Manufacturers liked to prove how good their bikes were and so nearly everyone entered them in competitions. Some raced them on special tracks, like Brooklands in the south of England, where they could show their top speed; others entered reliability trials which let the public see

Right from the start of motorcycling, women enjoyed bikes as much as men – even in long skirts and elegant hats. (Photo: EMAP Archives)

10

how strong the bikes were. In a reliability trial, the bikes would have to go over hundreds of miles of rough tracks, climbing the steepest hills and crossing deep rivers to try to win a Gold medal. Some of the best trials riders were women, who competed with the men and often beat them.

Then came the unemployment of the 1930s – the Great Depression. Few people had the money to buy motorcycles – they were more interested in feeding themselves! Many motorcycle manufacturers went out of business and others combined to make bigger companies. Now, bike makers were interested in producing machines at the cheapest possible price.

In 1939, the Second World War began and the British motorcycle

In the 1920s, huge crowds came to the Brooklands race track to see the heroes of the day race. The Brooklands track was like a huge concrete saucer and the best riders could do a lap at over 100 mph, even on these early bikes. (Photo: EMAP Archives)

Brooklands racers flat out at over 100 mph. (Photo: EMAP Archives)

11

The paddock at Brooklands where every motorcyclist dreamed of being 60 years ago. (Photo: EMAP Archives)

factories, like Matchless, Norton, BSA and Triumph were ordered to produce bikes for the army. The war went on for six years and thousands of bikes were made.

After the war, there were great shortages. People were willing to buy any bike they could find. Because they could sell all their products, the British manufacturers became lazy and arrogant. They didn't improve their bikes and their factories became old fashioned and used worn out machinery from before the war.

Because the British manufacturers were so big-headed, they didn't take the Japanese seriously. At first, the Japanese made only small bikes and many of them were not very good. Then they began racing their bikes and still everyone laughed at them. The bikes were slow and looked out of date. But the Japanese examined the best British, German and Italian bikes; photographed them and then went back to Japan and designed better motorcycles. They were determined to be the best!

The British factories had managers who were stupid and full of their own importance. They never rode the bikes their factories were making and they wouldn't listen to their customers. They were so big-headed that they still made fun of the Japanese bikes even when British motorcyclists were

The British engineers produced the cleverest motorcycle designs of the day, like this Triumph Ricardo (left) of the 20s and the beautiful 1000 cc Vincent V-twin (overleaf).

13

The British Bikes

The British bike makers produced every sort of motorcycle from commuter bikes to scrambles and road racing machines.

Today, British bikes are loved more than ever with huge shows where British bike enthusiasts meet together.

telling them how good they were. The British workers were more interested in arguing with the managers than in making good bikes, as they had done when British motorcycles were the best in the world. They no longer had pride in their work and British bikes became unreliable. They were so bad that riders used to make jokes about them breaking down and leaking oil.

The British motorcycle industry was not all bad. There were some fine engineers producing clever designs and there were still craftsmen who had pride in their work. In the old factories, there were workers who remembered when British bikes were the best in the world and they were broken-hearted when they saw what was happening.

But there were not enough of them and their warnings were ignored so the Japanese took over. First, Matchless ran out of money and then BSA and Triumph. The factories which had once made the bikes every motorcyclist in the world wanted to own were closed.

Now, the Japanese companies, like Honda, Suzuki and Yamaha are the names that everyone thinks of when they talk about bikes and the British makers were nearly destroyed – but not quite. In the next chapter, we will see what has happened to the Japanese and how the British manufacturers just managed to survive.

Modern Bikes

There are bikes made for pleasure and bikes for business. Bikes that old ladies ride to the shops and bikes for posing on in your best leathers. Whatever you want to do, there is a bike just for the job.

By the beginning of the 1970s, the British motorcycle industry was almost finished. The rest of the world was not much better either. In Germany, only BMW made many bikes and Harley-Davidson was the last manufacturer left in America. The Italian and Span-

ish factories also got into financial trouble as the Japanese made better and better bikes at prices which were actually cheaper each year.

Then, very slowly, the European manufacturers began to get back into business. The Japanese made the best bikes for ordinary motorcyclists. Their bikes were good value and worked well but riders who wanted a bike for a hobby were looking for something different – bikes which were not the same as everyone else rode. These

Mopeds are easy to ride and great fun.
(Photo: Honda (UK) Ltd.)

17

riders chose machines made by the famous old factories.

In Britain, Triumph, Matchless and Norton started making bikes again. Riders were proud to own bikes which had the same name on the petrol tank as had first appeared eighty years ago. They felt part of motorcycling history.

Now, British bikes have modern designs and are well made. The designers understand bikes and the workers are proud of the machines they make. Together, they produce good, reliable machines which are fun to own.

The only problem is that all the British and European manufacturers put together do not even make as many bikes as one of the Japanese factories. Together, the big four Japanese factories of Honda, Yamaha, Suzuki and Kawasaki make most of the world's motorcycles. By far the most important and successful bike manufacturer is Honda.

The Honda MTX is a great little bike on which to learn. (Photo: Honda (UK) Ltd.)

They can still do this because all the Japanese bikes are extremely well made and they are also very good value for money. You rarely find a Japanese bike which is unreliable or won't start.

The other reason the Japanese sell so many bikes is that they make every kind you can imagine.

If you want a simple moped which anybody can learn to ride in a few minutes then the Japanese can sell you one. Or would you prefer a sports bike which will take you up to 170 mph? Then all the Japanese make these as well. Let's have a look at some of the bikes which are on sale today.

The most basic bikes are mopeds. These machines have tiny 50 cc engines. They don't go very fast but are extremely easy to ride and use hardly any fuel. On the best mopeds, you only have to open the throttle to go and squeeze the brake to stop. That's all there is to riding. A good moped will easily cover over 100 miles on one gallon of petrol which means they are the most economical

form of motor transport.

Next comes the 125s. In Britain, you must ride these small bikes until you have passed your test. The small size of the engine means that while the bikes are fast enough to learn about riding, and are lots of fun, they are not so quick that they would be dangerous for a learner rider.

After training and passing a driving test, you can have a full motorcycle licence which means that you can ride any bike you want to – even a very fast one! Most riders go for a medium sized machine like a 400 cc bike. These machines have enough power to carry two people anywhere. They are fast enough to go down the motorway at 70 mph and have good handling and powerful brakes so that they are safe to ride. You can have a great time on a medium sized bike.

After you have got a lot of experience – and saved up a lot of money – you can have a Superbike. Some Superbikes have quite small engines – around 500 cc – while the biggest are 1300 cc. All the Superbikes are incredibly fast.

*The Honda CBR 600 is probably the finest all-round sports bike made today.
(Photo: Honda (UK) Ltd.)*

19

The fastest Superbikes will reach nearly 170 mph in just a few seconds and have special tyres and suspension so that they are safe at these speeds. They look just like the bikes used on the race tracks and they are capable of nearly the same speeds. For many motorcyclists, riding a Superbike is their dream.

The first Superbike was the Z1 Kawasaki. When it was first made this 900 cc bike was the fastest, strongest motorcycle ever mass-produced. It could cruise at 120 mph all day without ever getting tired but it was heavy and didn't handle very well.

Motorcyclists wanted even faster and bigger Superbikes and the Japanese tried hard to please their customers. Honda made the beautiful 6 cylinder CBX 1000, which is still one of the smoothest running motorcycles ever produced, and Suzuki arrived with the incredibly powerful GSX1100. The bikes got faster and faster and

although they were safe to ride, because the tyres, brakes and handling got better too, many riders found that these giant machines were not as much fun as smaller bikes.

So, the Japanese made smaller and lighter Superbikes, like the Honda CBR 600. This bike is light, very fast and handles so well that it is a dream to ride. For many riders, it is the ultimate Superbike.

The Japanese also make very specialised bikes. They produce machines for every form of motorcycle sport and even what they call recreational machines for riding on the beach or for cruising down to your local hamburger shop and just looking cool and relaxed.

Whatever kind of bike you choose, it must be fun, whether this is just looking cool or super sporty in your brightly coloured leathers. More than anything else, bikes are about having a good time.

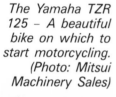

The Yamaha TZR 125 – A beautiful bike on which to start motorcycling. (Photo: Mitsui Machinery Sales)

Parts of the Bike

Now, let's have a look at the different parts of a bike and how they work. As we read in Chapter One, the first motorcycles were often made by pedal cycle manufacturers so even today, we still use many of the same words to describe pedal bikes and motorcycles. You will probably already be familiar with a lot of the terms in this chapter.

The main part of the motorcycle is the frame. This is usually made from steel tubing and is very strong. A well designed frame does not twist or flex. Twisting and flexing can make the bike wobble on corners, or sometimes even in a straight line, causing bad handling. No rider wants a bad handling bike.

The wheels of the bike are connected to the frame by the suspension. The suspension moves up and down as the bike goes over bumps in the road so that the rider is not shaken about and the frame does not twist. The suspension must work efficiently

(Photo: Mitsui Machinery Sales)

Front brake lever

Clutch lever

Saddle

Petrol tank

Frame

Rear brake

Exhaust pipe   Gear lever

Swinging arm

Front brake.

Front forks

if the bike is going to handle well. Without suspension, the wheels would leave the ground when they hit bumps and this could be very dangerous.

At the front of the bike are the forks. These look like long, thin tubes and as the front wheel hits a bump one tube is pushed up inside the other so that the ride is smooth.

The back wheel is held in a piece of metal shaped like a letter "U", laying flat, called the swinging arm. This moves up and down when the rear wheel hits a bump. It is controlled by suspension, just like the front forks only with much shorter tubes. The suspension at the back of the bike, controlling the movement of the swinging-arm, is called the rear shock. There can be one rear shock or two but they both do the same job of keeping the rear wheel on the ground and making the bike more comfortable for the rider.

Each wheel has a brake. Now, most bikes have powerful disc brakes which can stop the bike quickly. On the right-hand side of the handlebar there is a lever which controls the front brake. When you squeeze it, the front brake works. The front brake is always the most powerful one and it is the best brake for stopping the bike quickly.

The back brake is controlled by a lever under the rider's right foot. When the lever is pushed down the rear brake is operated. You have to be careful not to press down too hard on the rear brake or you can cause the bike to skid.

The rider sits on the bike's saddle. Usually, there is room for two people. In front of the saddle is the petrol tank which holds the fuel for the engine.

When you turn the petrol tap on, the fuel flows into the carburettor. This is a very important part of the bike. The carburettor mixes petrol and air in exactly the right amounts for the engine to burn. You will often hear riders talking about carburation problems. This means that their carburettor is not working properly and is making the engine run badly.

The engine needs clean air if it is to run well. Behind the carburettor is a box which contains the air filter. Air has to pass through the air filter before it reaches the carburettor. The air filter removes all the dirt so that the engine has clean air. In the next chapter, we will look at how the different kinds of engine use the air when it finally reaches them.

Engines

In this chapter we will look at four-stroke and two-stroke engines – the main kinds of motors bikes use – and we will also talk about gearboxes.

There are many different makes of motorcycle engine but nearly all are either two-strokes or four-strokes. Let's have a look at two-stroke engines first. They use a mixture of petrol and oil. The mixture starts at the bottom of the engine and then goes up the cylinder barrel through passages called ports. Finally, it is burnt in the top of the engine between the piston and cylinder head. As the fuel passes through the engine, the oil lubricates all the parts and helps keep them cool.

A two-stroke engine produces plenty of power but it uses a lot of fuel. Many racing bikes have two-stroke engines because they produce such good power. They are also quite light too, which is very important for racing.

In a four-stroke engine, the fuel goes into the top of the engine through valves in the cylinder head. These are shaped like plates on the ends of long sticks, only much smaller. When the valve is pushed away from the cylinder head, the petrol and air

A twin cylinder four-stroke engine. (Photo: Honda (UK) Ltd.)

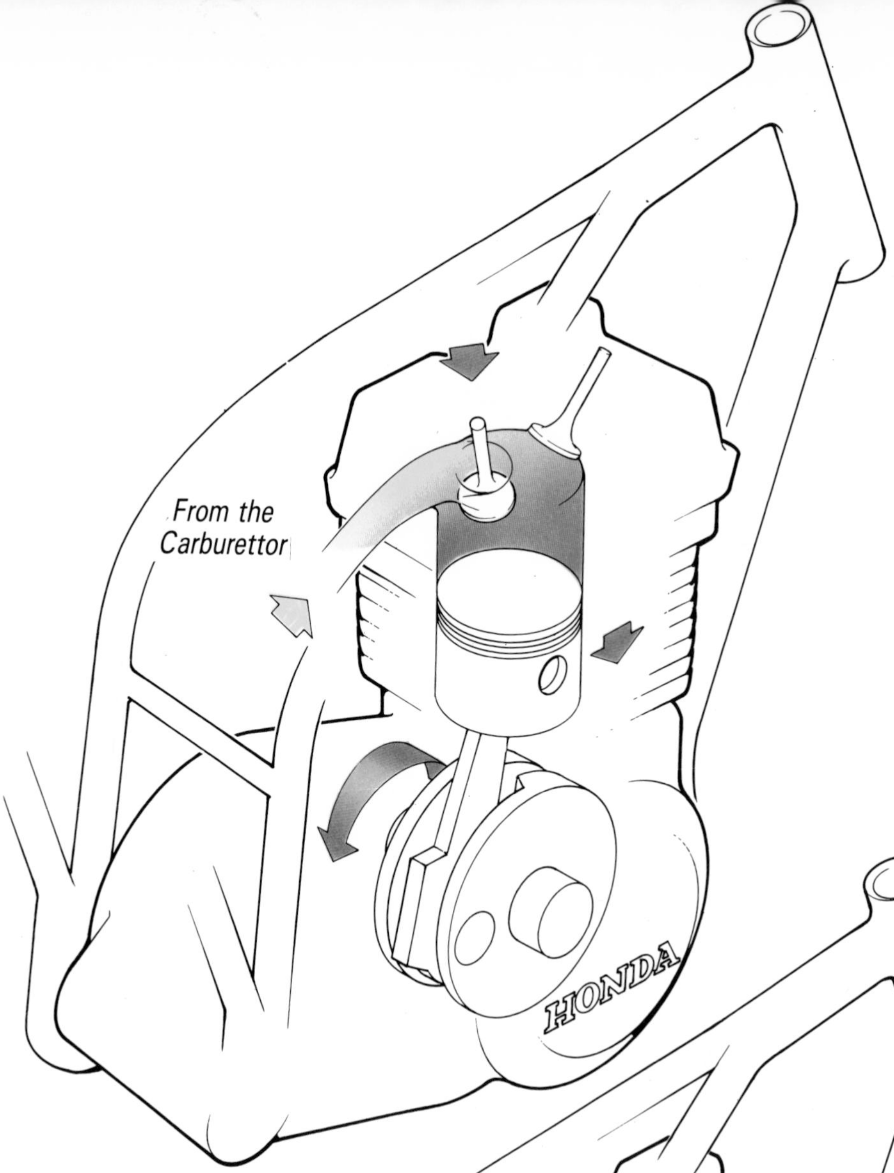

4-stroke engine,
Induction.
(Adrian Carter)

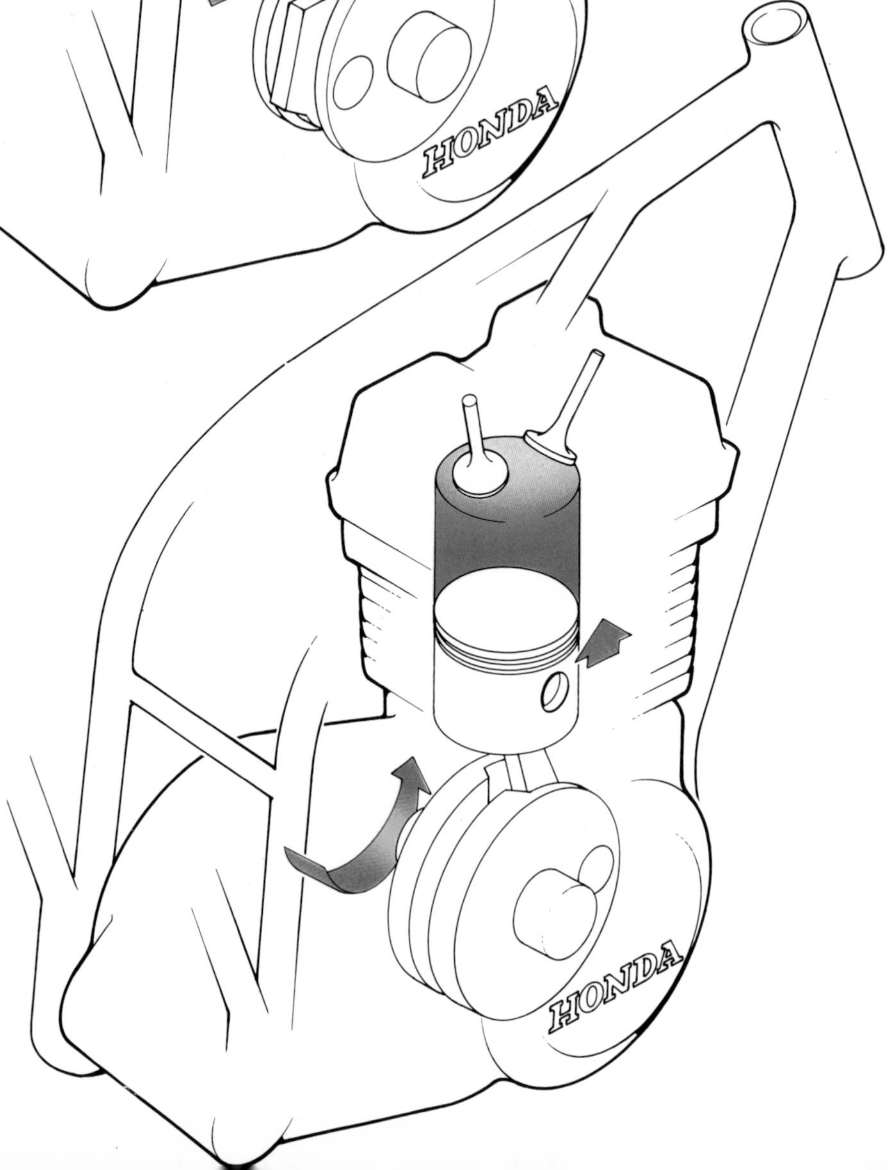

From the
Carburettor

HONDA

24

4-stroke engine,
Compression.
(Adrian Carter)

HONDA

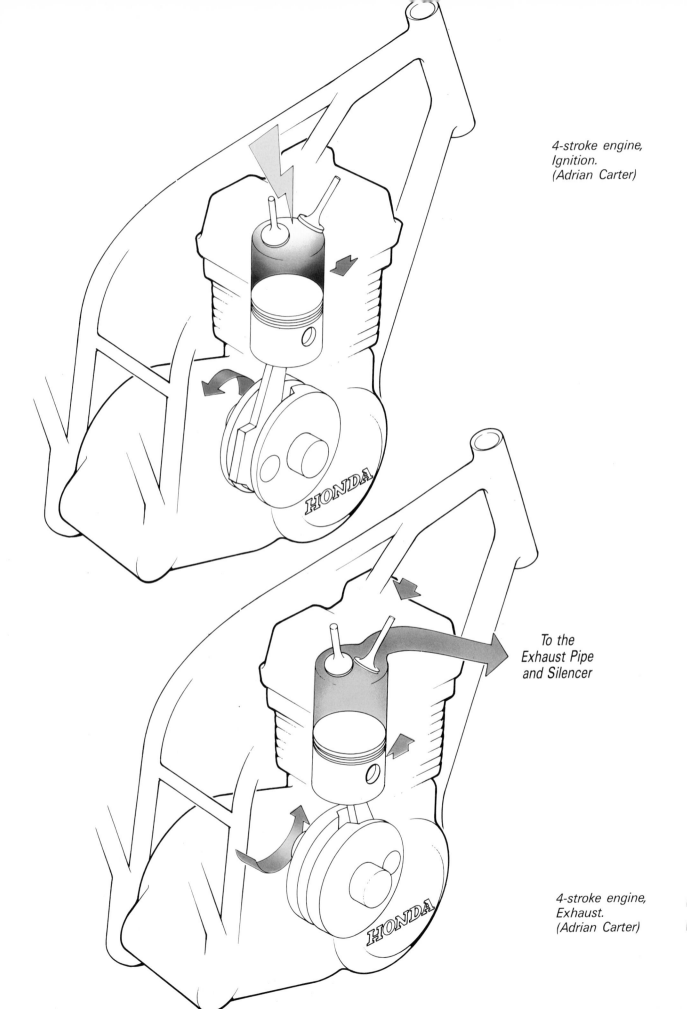

4-stroke engine,
Ignition.
(Adrian Carter)

To the
Exhaust Pipe
and Silencer

4-stroke engine,
Exhaust.
(Adrian Carter)

25

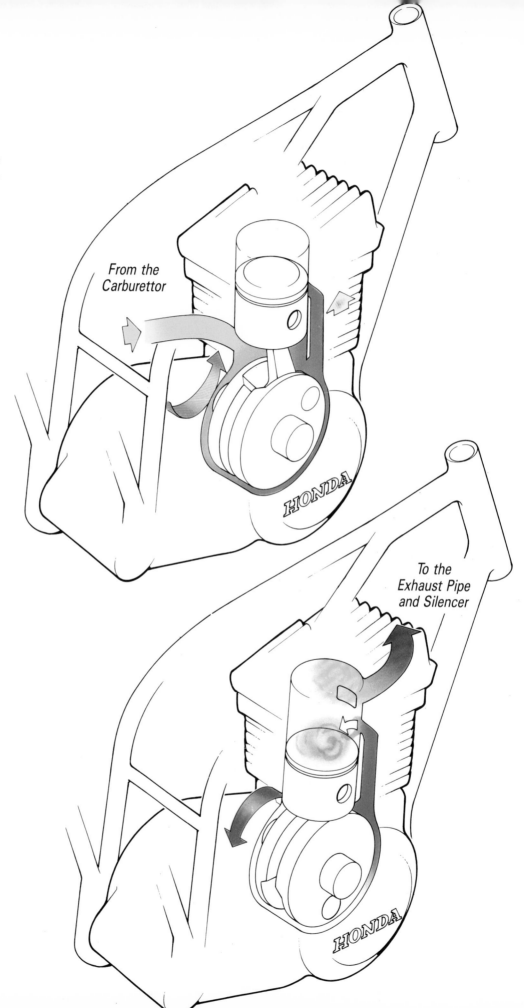

2-stroke engine, Induction and Compression prior to ignition. (Adrian Carter)

From the Carburettor

To the Exhaust Pipe and Silencer

2-stroke engine, Exhaust and Transfer phase. (Adrian Carter)

26

can get in and after the fuel has been used, another valve opens and the burnt gases escape. The valve which lets the fuel in is called the inlet valve and when it opens, the petrol and air go straight into the top of the engine where they are exploded by the spark plug. Then the exhaust valve opens and all the burnt gas rushes out of the engine to make room for more fuel to be ignited by the spark plug. All this happens many thousands of times a minute! If you could see all the moving parts inside the engine they would just be a blur.

When the fuel is burnt, there is an explosion which pushes the piston down. The piston is connected to the bottom of the engine by a rod and this turns the crankshaft, just like you pushing the pedals of your bike. But you know that you would be wasting your time if you turned the pedals and there was no chain! It is the chain which connects your pedalling to the bike's wheel and makes you go.

A motorcycle is nearly the same. The engine is connected to a gearbox first and then the gearbox has a chain going to the rear wheel. The gearbox lets the bike go faster or slower and helps it climb hills. A low gear is used for starting off and for climbing hills and a high gear is used for going fast. When you see a rider on an open road or on the motorway he will always be in top gear. Most bikes have five gears and when the rider is cruising, he will use fifth gear.

To change gear, the rider has to first pull in the clutch. This is controlled by a lever on the left-hand side of the handlebar. When the lever is pulled in, the engine is disconnected from the gearbox for a moment while the gears are changed. It is like you free-wheeling on a pedal cycle. The gears are changed by a lever under the rider's left foot. You press it down to change to a lower gear and lift it up to change to a higher gear.

When you ride a bike there's always plenty to do. There's something for the rider's left foot to operate and his right and both hands too! You never have time to get bored riding a bike. And when you can ride well, there is a tremendous satisfaction from making every part of the bike work just as you want.

A modern two-stroke engine. (Photo: Honda (UK) Ltd.)

Buying a Bike

Buying your first bike is one of the most exciting things you will ever do. It's also one of the most worrying! Buy the wrong bike and all your hard-earned savings will disappear and you can be left with a wreck which won't do anything except remind you about the money you have wasted. Buying a bike needs a lot of care!

The first thing to decide is whether

The front forks on this bike are useless because rust has ruined the fork leg. It will now be impossible to stop oil leaks.

you are going to buy a bike from a motorcycle dealer or from a private person. There are good points about both ways – and there are problems too.

Bikes are advertised privately in the local newspapers and also in the motorcycle press. Because everyone who advertises a bike wants to sell it, the advertisements will make the bike sound as good as possible. Few people will tell actual lies but they might not tell the whole truth either. For example, someone might say in their advertisement that their bike is, "an excellent runner" – which means that the motor is in good condition. But they won't tell you that the bike needs new tyres or that the brakes are worn out. You will have to find that out for yourself. It would take a saint to tell you all the things which would make you **not** want to buy his machine – and not many saints ride bikes!

When you buy a bike privately, the responsibility for deciding its condition is entirely up to you. This means that you must really understand bikes, or have someone with you who is an expert, to be sure that the machine you are buying is a good one. The person selling the bike will probably give you a receipt which says, "Sold as seen and approved." This means that if you find anything wrong with the bike when you get it home, then it's tough luck. You have bought the bike and no matter what is wrong with it, you're stuck with it!

But there are advantages in buying a bike privately. If you understand exactly what you are doing, or have got someone with you who really knows bikes, you can often get a real bargain. A person selling a bike privately does not have to make a profit, like a dealer, so he will usually ask less for his bike. Some people need money quickly, or get fed up with their bike and want a new one, and they will often sell their bikes cheaply too.

So what do you look for when you are buying a bike? You really need to be an expert to be sure of what you are doing but even someone who has just started riding can get quite a good idea of what the bike is like – but you **must** take time to think about what you are doing.

The first thing to do is just to look at the bike and ask yourself, "Does this bike look as if it has been cared for? Does it look scruffy or has it been cleaned and looked after?" The appearance of the bike will tell you a lot about its owner.

Now, let's think about some of the more definite things to look for. If you follow these rules, you will at least look as if you are an expert and perhaps the seller will tell you things about the bike he would not normally have mentioned.

First, look at the wheels. Are the tyres bald or nearly worn out? If they are, they will be expensive to replace. Are the spokes loose? Does the wheel rim have any deep marks in it where it might have been damaged in an accident?

You can also tell whether a bike has been in an accident by looking at the indicators, the clutch and brake levers and the footrests. If any of these have been damaged, then the bike will have at least fallen over but it might also have been in an accident. If it has been crashed, then there is a good chance that the frame and suspension will have been weakened too. You don't want to be riding a bike which has been damaged like this.

The bike's owner will not let you ride the bike but you can check that all the gears are working by changing gear with the engine stopped and the bike on its centre-stand. Get a friend to move the back wheel a little bit between each gear change to let the gears engage. Go from first to fifth gear and then back again, counting the number of gear changes. Don't forget to find neutral, which comes between first and second gear.

Ask the seller to start the bike. It should start easily and the engine should run quietly. If it won't start for him, you can bet your last penny it won't start for you, so stay away from

There is a lot of corrosion on this front brake caliper. This looks so bad that it could be dangerous. A bike without good brakes will kill you!

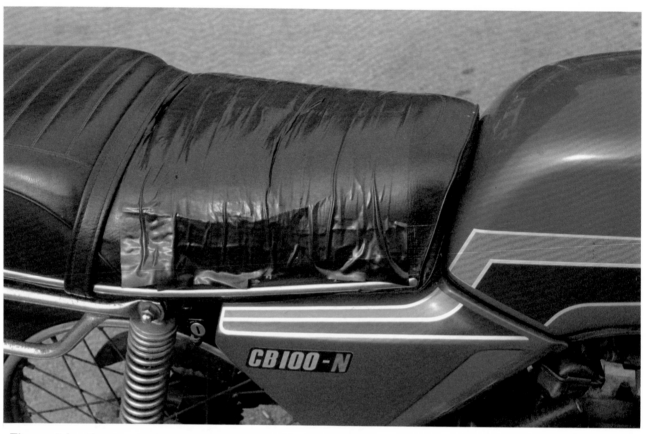

The seat has been ripped and stuck together with black tape. What does this tell you about the bike's last owner?

it! The engine should be quiet. If there are any funny noises coming from the engine, leave it alone. All bikes should be quiet and if the exhaust is noisy it will need replacing. Only idiots run bikes with noisy exhausts because unless the silencer is working properly, the engine can easily be damaged. Noisy exhausts are illegal too!

Next, check that the suspension is working smoothly by putting the front brake on and gently bouncing the bike up and down. The front forks should move smoothly, without any stiffness or clanking noises. Carefully bounce on the saddle to check the rear suspension. Always be careful and gentle when looking at someone else's bike or they might bounce up and down on you!

Check that all the electrical gear is working properly. The lights should work on main beam and dip and the horn should be clear. Put your hand over the headlamp when the engine is running and then switch on the lights. If they go much brighter as the engine is revved up, then the battery is probably in poor condition. New batteries are not very expensive but there could also be problems with the bike's generator and these can cost a fortune to repair. All these things will affect how much you pay for the bike.

You don't have to pay the price the seller puts in the advertisement. Without being bad-mannered, you can point out the things which are wrong with the bike and ask him to reduce the price of the machine. If he won't then you can look at another bike. It's as simple as that.

You can do just the same thing when you buy a bike from a dealer. The only difference – and it is a big one

– is that the dealer will have to tell you the truth about the bike. If he says the engine is in good condition, it has to be in good condition – by law. All dealers have to sell bikes which are of merchantable quality. This means that they have to do the job they are sold for. If you buy a bike from a dealer and when you take it home, you find something badly wrong, then the dealer will have to repair the fault or give you your money back.

But the law is not the main reason a dealer will want to keep you happy. Unlike a private seller, the dealer wants you to come back and buy bikes from him again and again. Another reason for going to a dealer is that most of the people in the motorcycle business love bikes. They will want you to have a bike which will be safe and give you a lot of pleasure so that you will become a biker like them.

They will also be able to help with credit facilities, insurance and servicing – all of which we will look at in the next chapter.

*The tyre on this bike is illegal and **very** dangerous. It will need replacing before the bike can be sold.*

At best, bent control levers show that the bike has been dropped on its side or has been crashed and the frame damaged. Think before you buy.

Ready for the Road

Buying a bike from a motorcycle dealer is the easiest, and safest, way to begin motorcycling. Not only will you be sure of having a machine which is roadworthy but the dealer will also help with things like getting a provisional driving licence, insurance and credit facilities. All these are easy to deal with when you know what to do but can be worrying at first.

Before the dealer can help you, he needs to know what sort of bike you want and what you intend doing with it. New bikes are great to own because they are shiny new and right up to date but they are expensive. A better choice might be a good second-hand machine.

If possible, it is better to have saved up the money for your bike and then you can buy it without any credit. Credit means that someone lends you the money – and they won't do this for free!

There are several types of credit but the most common is a bank loan. How much the loan will cost is called the APR. The longer you borrow the money for, then the more it will cost you. Also, all APR's are not the same and some are more expensive than others. The higher the APR, the more the loan will cost you. For example, an APR of 29% means that the money that you borrow will cost you more than a loan with an APR of 25%. Always look for the lowest APR. You can get a loan through a dealer or from your bank.

Training is fun.

If you are under 18, then an adult will have to guarantee the loan. This means that if you don't pay, the person who guaranteed the loan will be held responsible.

Many lenders have schemes where you can take out insurance against losing your job or being taken ill and this means that your loan will still be re-paid even if something goes wrong.

When you are 16, you can ride a moped. These are small bikes powered by a 50 cc engine. They are not as much fun as a real motorcycle but they are useful for gaining experience.

At 17, you can have a real motorcycle but again it will be restricted in size and power so that you can learn to ride safely. These bikes cannot have an engine bigger than 125 cc and their engine must not produce more than 12 bhp. This is enough power to be fun but not so much that the bikes are difficult to ride.

There are a huge range of "learner" 125s. You can have water-cooled street scramblers like Honda's MTX 125 or the same engine in a chassis which looks just like a road-racer. These are the machines for the keen biker but some riders just want to use their bikes for getting to work or college and they might choose one of the little scooters, like the Vision. All the learner bikes are very safe and easy to ride and if you buy a machine from a dealer, you know it will be reliable too.

Before you can ride your bike, you need a provisional licence but in order to validate it you have to go on a compulsory training course. This takes place on some area off the road, where there is no other traffic, and to which your bike will have to be transported. The instructor will help you become familiar with the bike's controls and show you how to ride it safely. You will also be told a little bit about looking after your bike. It's all a lot of fun and you will be with a group of other learners so you can

Your dealer can help you with all the essential form filling.

Getting to know your new mechanical friend.

have a laugh together.

When you pass the course, you will be given a certificate which will validate your provisional licence. You can then ride your bike on the road, with all the other traffic, but before you do, there are three very important things to check – especially is you have bought your bike privately. First and most important, you must have insurance. This means that if you have an accident and injure someone else or damage their property, the insurance company will pay the costs. It is an **extremely** serious crime to ride without insurance.

Most learners have third party insurance. This means that if you are in an accident the insurance company will pay for the damage to the other person's vehicle but not your own. Of course, if the accident is not your fault, your bike will be repaired by the person who damaged it. As you get more experience, the insurance becomes less expensive and you can have a comprehensive policy which means that no matter whose fault the accident was you will get your bike repaired. However, this kind of insurance is usually too expensive for beginners.

You will also have to make sure that your bike has road-tax, and an MoT certificate, if it is more than three years old. Unfortunately, everyone has to pay

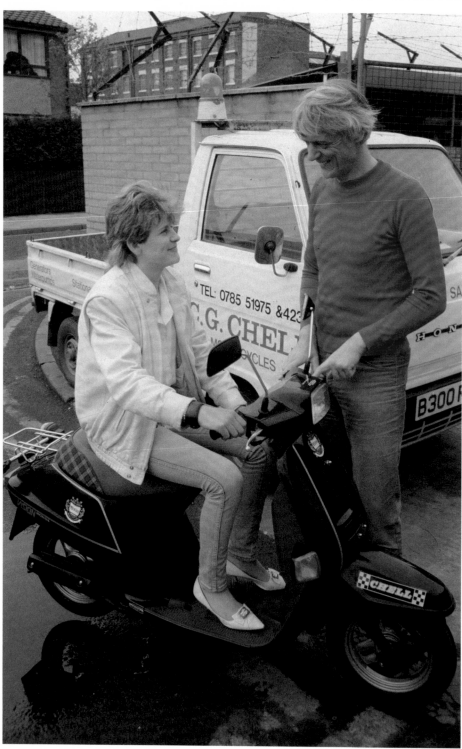

road tax no matter what they drive. An MoT certificate is given when your bike has been examined by a qualified tester to make sure that it is safe. All vehicles over three years old need an MoT certificate. Your dealer will get both of these for you.

Last, but most important of all, you will need a helmet. It is illegal to ride a bike if you are not wearing a helmet and very stupid too!

You can now ride on the road but you will also have to apply for a motorcycle test. You have two years in which to take and pass the test, otherwise you will be off the road for a year before you can reapply.

In the test, you won't have to do any fancy riding or be asked trick questions. The tester will just be interested to see if you can ride safely and sensibly so that you won't be a danger to yourself or other road users. You will have to follow a route which will be explained to you by the tester while he follows you on his bike. He will watch that you can control your bike properly and that you treat other vehicles sensibly.

After he has watched you ride for a time, he will bring you back to the test centre and ask you a few questions about the highway code – again for your safety and for other road users. It is no good to anyone if someone is driving around who doesn't know the rules that everyone else is obeying!

Most riders should pass their full driving test on the first attempt because it is quite straightforward if you ride sensibly and safely. Then you will be given the magic slip of paper which says that you have passed and you can get your full licence. Now there is nowhere in the world that you cannot ride your bike and nowhere that you cannot go. Now you are a real motorcyclist.

Your dealer will always give you honest, accurate advice.

Clothing

To keep warm and dry, the first motor-cyclists used to have to dress up in great big coats and leather boots, as if they were going on an expedition to the North Pole. Now, bike clothing is smart, comfortable and most of all, safe.

The most important part of a rider's equipment is his helmet. Most riders never need a helmet except to keep their ears warm but it is like a pilot's parachute. When that chance in a million comes and you do need it, the helmet has got to work properly. Whatever else you try to save money on, buy the best possible helmet: it could save your life one day.

All helmets in Britain have to be tested for safety by the British Standards Institution – or BSI for short. They set the safety standards for helmets with two numbers which are BS6658B and BS6658A. Both are extremely strict standards and helmets must be very good to pass them. The strictest test is BS6658A which is the toughest test for helmets in the world. The helmets used by racing riders have to pass this test. A helmet which has passed BS6658 is now the only new one that can be sold legally although those meeting the older standards can still be worn.

Helmets are mainly made from two materials. One is glass fibre and the other polycarbonate. Both materials are very safe but if you have a helmet made from polycarbonate, you must not put stickers on it or try to paint it. If you do, the helmet's shell can be damaged.

Even if you have a fibre-glass helmet, it is better to leave it alone because a helmet is too important to use for experiments.

Some helmets are extremely expensive but remember, you might be paying for beautiful paint work and not the protection it gives to you. Always look for the BSI stamp which will tell you exactly the safety of the helmet.

There are full face and open face helmets. The full-face give better protection to the front of the rider's face but some people feel very closed in wearing them. If you can get used to the feeling, a full-face helmet is better.

When you buy a helmet, choose the smallest size which does not hurt your head. A helmet which is too big will move around and can be dangerous. Always buy a helmet which is a firm fit but does not squeeze your head.

When you wear your helmet, always

AGV helmet showing BSI kite marks and ACU Gold label.

keep the strap as tight as possible. Nearly all the riders who have head injuries are hurt because their helmet came off.

Your eyes need just as much protection as your head. Goggles worn with an open face helmet, or a visor used with a full-face helmet, will both give good protection – if you wear them. At first, it feels a little bit strange having something in front of your eyes so you have to make yourself always ride with your goggles or visor down. In two or three weeks, it will feel strange **not** to have your eyes protected. If you look at an expert biker, whether they are riding on the road or the track, you will see that they always have some kind of eye protection. All goggles and visors must have a BSI number marked on them. This will be BS 4110 followed by the letters X, Y or Z. X gives the least protection and Z the most.

There are so many ways of keeping dry and warm that you will find it is difficult to know where to start. Motorcycling clothing today is smart, clean and it works too. Probably the best choice for the beginner is a two-piece suit. Except in the winter, you will usually be able to ride just in your jacket, saving the trousers for the bad weather. When you go to buy a suit there are several things you should look for. First, check how the seams are covered. Rain can get blown in so the seams should be either welded – where the plastic is melted together so it is completely waterproof – or have a protective tape inside. If you gently squeeze the jacket along the seams, you can usually feel the tape – if it is there!

Next, look at the zips, the collar and cuffs. The zips should be strong. The jacket will get a lot of blowing about and a weak zip will soon break. The collar and cuffs should be able to be closed tightly, so that the wind will not

blow in. Like the zip, they should be strongly made too.

The insulating material is what keeps the jacket warm. This is the padding inside the jacket. A warm jacket does not have to have very thick padding. Modern jackets use material like *Thinsulate* which can be very warm without being bulky.

Aluminium foil is another good way of keeping warm and the dealer will tell you if the jacket has this in the lining.

A good glove should be waterproof and comfortable. Always test they fit as you grip the handlebars.

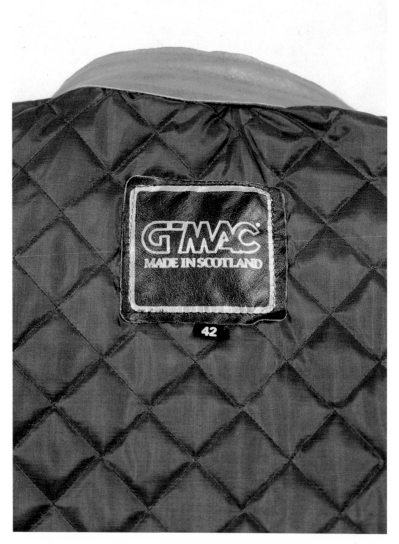

Suit linings need not be thick and heavy to be warm. This quilted lining is comfortable and retains all the heat.

warm and dry but they would be so bulky that you would never be able to feel what the bike was doing. You must buy a pair of leather gloves. Plastic ones are just a dangerous joke and useless for bike riding no matter how smart they look. Try to buy gloves which the dealer says are waterproof and make sure that you try holding the 'bars on a bike before you buy them. If they don't feel comfortable, don't buy them.

At one time, everyone wore leather boots but now many riders use Derry boots which are made from a strong rubber. The advantage with Derry boots is that they are waterproof and much cheaper than leather boots but they don't protect your feet as well as leather if you do have an accident. Even so, many riders wear them because they are so comfortable.

Most riders want a leather jacket as soon as they start riding. Leather looks very smart, and it does give you the best protection, but it is only a little water resistant and leather jackets are not very warm either. When you have bought a waterproof suit, a leather jacket, or better still, a full set of leathers is nice to have as well. Then you can wear your waterproof clothes over your leathers in bad weather and this way you will have the best of both worlds.

Like all the rest of your clothing, you must think carefully before buying leathers. Never buy a leather jacket made from sheep skin. This leather is too soft for motorcycle clothing and will tear easily if you have an accident. The best leather suits are made from cow or goat skin. Anything else is a waste of money.

Some of the very best leathers are made in Scotland by the British G-MAC company. They will even make you a set of leathers to fit your own special body shape with each

The same rules apply when buying a pair of trousers. Make sure that the trouser seat is strong because you spend a lot of time sitting down on a bike! Look at the bottom of the trouser legs and see if they can be buckled tightly round your boots so they don't flap about in the wind. You often find *Thinsulate* and aluminium foil used for trouser linings too.

Gloves are important because they must keep your hands warm at the same time as being thin enough to let you feel the controls. It would be easy to make gloves which were always piece being carefully measured before it is sewn together so that the suit fits you exactly. Racers have leathers made like this because they are so comfortable but they are expensive too!

A good set of leathers will finish off your bike gear which will keep you warm, dry and safe – as well as looking super-smart too!

Seams need to be welded or taped to be waterproof.

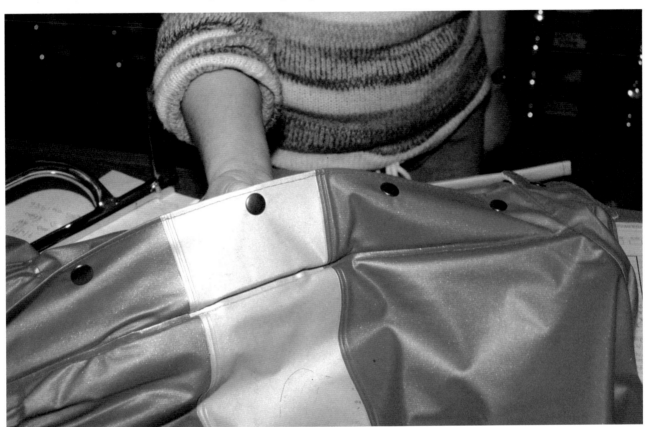

Caring for Your Bike

Carefully wipe all the oil from the dipstick with a clean rag or tissue before checking it.

One of the best things about motorcycling is that you can look after all the normal maintenance on your bike yourself. Caring for your own bike not only makes it safer for you to ride but it also becomes worth more when you come to sell it. Most of all, when you look after the bike yourself, you really become friends with it!

Let's begin with the engine because if it's not looked after, it won't run and you won't go anywhere at all! All engines depend on having oil – it's like their blood and without it, they will die just as quickly as we would without our blood. If you have a four-stroke bike, there will be a dipstick on the bottom of the engine, probably on the right-hand side. Check the oil when the bike has been stood for a few minutes and is on its centre stand. This is because when the engine is run, the oil will be spread about inside and it is difficult to tell accurately how much is in there. First, unscrew the dipstick. Wipe all the oil off the dipstick with a clean rag or tissue and put the dipstick back. If the oil comes above the top mark, there is too much oil in your engine and this might make the motor leak. This is bad for the motor. But if the oil is below the bottom mark, then this is worse because it means that the engine is short of oil.

If the motor needs more oil, pour a little at a time into the engine until it nearly reaches the top mark. Every time you check the oil level, wipe the dipstick with a clean rag. When you think that

40

the oil level is correct, run the motor for a few minutes and then have a final check.

Just as important is to change the oil whenever the manufacturer says it should be changed. Only use the best oil like Castrol GTX. Putting a cheap oil in your engine would be like using someone else's worn out blood!

On a two-stroke, checking the oil is much easier. There will be an oil-tank on the bike, probably under the saddle. Unscrew the filler cap and make sure that the tank is nearly full. If it is low, fill it up with a good quality two-stroke oil like Castrol Super TT. Never put a two-stroke oil in a four-stroke engine, or the other way about. Oil companies like Castrol make special oils for two-strokes and four-strokes and they are completely different and must never be mixed. Whether you have a two-stroke or a four-stroke engine, check the oil level at least once a week.

Now, let's have a look at the brakes. First, put the bike on its centre-stand and get someone to press down on the saddle so that the front wheel comes in the air. Spin the front wheel. It should move easily and not catch on the disc. Put the front brake on and the wheel should stop instantly.

You can do the same

thing to the rear wheel. If you have a drum brake on the back, make sure that the brake arm does not go past 90° when the brake is fully on. If it does, then the brake shoes are worn and you should get a mechanic to

Checking the oil level on a two-stroke.

41

change them immediately.

Next, go to the front brake lever and make sure that there is no brake fluid leaking from the brake pipe, where it joins the master cylinder. You can see if there is enough brake fluid in the master cylinder by looking at the reservoir at the same time. Like the dipstick, there will be two lines on the reservoir and the brake fluid should come between them. Don't try to change brake fluid yourself but go to a bike shop and ask the mechanic for help.

The next most important thing is the tyres. Every manufacturer works out the correct tyre pressures for each bike with the help of the tyre makers like Avon. If the tyres are too soft or too hard they will not grip properly and will be dangerous. They will also wear out too fast and this is expensive.

Unscrew the dust cover on the tyre valve and put the pressure gauge firmly on the valve. Do it quickly and no air will escape. Check the pressure two or three times to make sure that you haven't made a mistake. If there is too much air, you can press the valve in with the end of the tyre gauge and let some out. Only do this for a couple of seconds because air escapes very quickly. If the pressure is too low, you will need a foot pump or an air-line at a garage to put air in. Like the oil, check the tyre pressures at least once a week.

There are several other checks that you can do to keep your bike running well. First, make sure that the clutch lever does not have too much play in it. This means that there should be about 3 mm of gap before you feel the pressure of pulling in the clutch. If the gap is too big or too small the clutch won't operate properly and you might damage the gearbox as well. You can adjust it with the screw which is next to the clutch lever.

The chain must be at the correct tension for it to work safely and well. This means that it mustn't be too tight or too slack. Put the bike on the centre-stand and then feel how tight the chain is with your finger. Try to lift the chain in the middle of its bottom run. You should be able to lift it about 20 mm. If you can lift it more than this, it is too slack. Any less it is too tight and will damage the engine. You can

Check the tyre pressures. Do this every week at least.

adjust the chain yourself but you really need an experienced motorcyclist to show you how to do it the first time.

For safety, chains should always be riveted together. This means that two ends are joined together permanently. Some chains are joined by a split link but this is not as safe as riveting. if your chain has a split link it is **very** important that the link is put on correctly. The spring on the split link should face outwards, away from the tyre and the closed end of the spring **must** always face the engine when it is on the top run of the chain. If the split link is not fitted like this, it might come off and the chain will fly about and wreck the engine. It could also stop the rear wheel from turning and might make you crash.

Never fit a cheap chain to a bike. It can be dangerous. Only use a high quality chain like Renolds, which will last longer and be much safer.

When you have checked the chain tension, it needs to be oiled. Ordinary oil is no good for this job. You must use a special chain oil like Castrol Chain Lube. Squirt this on the inside of the chain as you slowly spin the rear wheel. Then wait for five minutes for the oil to thicken before riding the bike.

As you are riding along, get used to the idea of listening for any

unusual noises your bike makes. As you get to know your bike, you will be able to recognise the normal noises it makes when it is working well and happily. If any of the noises change, don't ignore them but find out what

Checking the chain tension. Don't have the chain too tight or you will damage the engine. Don't run it too slack either.

Lubing the chain. Only use a specially designed chain lube. Lube the chain every week and leave the bike for five minutes to allow the chain lube to dry before you ride the bike.

they are. If you do this, you can often find a problem before it damages your bike.

To look after your bike, you will need some basic tools. Unfortunately, the ones which come with a bike are usually rubbish so as soon as you can afford it, buy some decent ones. You will need a simple set of metric ring spanners and open-ended spanners as well as a pair of pliers and two or three screwdrivers. The open ended spanners are for tightening and slackening nuts which are hard to get at, but you should only use them when you can't get a ring spanner to fit. A ring spanner always gives a much better grip on the nut and protects it from damage. A good set of Britool spanners will last you a complete lifetime!

Your bike will keep its value if you clean it regularly. First, wash all the dirt off with warm, soapy water. If you use a power wash, be careful not to aim the jet at the carburettor or the electrical system. When the bike is clean, the paintwork can be polished with a wax cleaner and the chrome cleaned with one of the special chrome cleaners. As you clean the polish off, look out for any loose nuts or bolts and also for any cracks which you might find in places like the mudguards or the side-panels. Keeping your eyes open as you polish can save you a lot of money and it might even help you avoid an accident one day!

Dream a Bike

Whatever your dream bike, you can have it. If you want to cruise around the town, you can ride a relaxed street machine. If you want to ride across the Sahara desert, then there's a bike for the job. Or if you would rather relive the olden days, there are the classics to ride.

From the moment you first ride a bike, it's fun. But when you have got a full licence, and a few miles of road experience, bike riding is like entering a dream world. The difference between cars and bikes is that most cars are used for moving people about from one place to another. They are designed to do this quickly, efficiently and as cheaply as possible. Most car drivers just want their vehicle to work for them – they don't expect them to be fun too!

Bikes are completely different. Most bike riders want their machines to be part of them. Yes, they have got to work efficiently – a bike which keeps breaking down is no good to anyone – but more than anything else, they've got to be exciting. Many bike riders drive a car to get them to work and back and have a bike for the evenings

Harley-Davidson make some of the best street cruisers.

and weekends, when they start to live. Let's have a look at some of the fantastic machines you can ride once you become a motorcyclist.

Some of the best looking bikes are the street and custom machines. The custom bikes copy the choppers which were first made on the west coast of America, in California. Here the weather is usually sunny, dry and warm. In the 1950s, the riders there became bored with the big, heavy American bikes which were on sale so they made them lighter and began to modify them with lots of chrome and fantastic paint work. They called their bikes choppers and soon there were thousands of these bikes just cruising

(Left) Some riders like to customise their bikes like this immaculate Vetter Triumph.

Yamaha make the meanest, toughest trail bike of all – the mighty Ténéré.

(Photo: Mitsui Machinery Sales)

You can go anywhere on a trail bike.

around California, not going very fast but having a good time.

The first choppers were based on Harley-Davidson bikes. These bikes had big V twin engines which made a lovely rumbling noise from the short exhaust pipes. Later, the Japanese manufacturers copied the Harley-Davidson style and made bikes with V twin engines, lots of chrome and fantastic paint work too. Probably the best of these custom bikes is Suzuki's 1300 cc Invader. Just the thing for looking cool and relaxed – even if you are not in California.

Some riders liked the idea of street cruising but didn't like the chopper look. They made street bikes which were low and light but have powerful engines. They are not very good for travelling long distances but are just the thing for making a big impression at the disco!

Other bikers would find street machines a joke. Their idea of a good bike is one which can go for thou-sands of miles without the slightest trouble. These are the touring riders and their bikes are just as fantastic as the street machines. Probably the best touring bike in the world is the Honda Aspencade. This bike has a huge six cylinder engine with five forward gears and even a reverse! It has a massive fairing and windscreen which keep the rain and wind right off the rider, and a saddle like an armchair. Behind the pillion passenger are pan-niers, like suitcases, and of course the rider has his own stereo built into the bike.

An Aspencade costs more than a medium sized car but no car can match the luxury of this bike. You can ride it all day without a break and when you stop, you can be sure that there will be a crowd of people admir-ing your bike. You don't get that with a car!

Aspencades are big, heavy and lux-urious – like a top-class hotel on two wheels. There are a lot of riders who would rather drive a car than ride a bike like this. These are the Superbike fans. Superbikes are the race horses of the motorcycle world. Usually, they will be four cylinder bikes ranging in size from 500cc to 1100cc. The engine can be two or four stroke but whatever design they use they will be fast! All the Superbikes will be capable of over 160 mph and will be able to go from a standstill to 100 mph in seven

or eight seconds! Superbikes are only for very experienced riders but even though they are so fast, they are not dangerous. All the Superbikes were developed from road racing machines and this means that not only are their engines good but so are their brakes and handling. Superbikes can go very quickly but they also stop just as fast and their handling is the safest of any bike.

Long distance touring is tremendous fun on a bike.

Dream A Bike

Superbikes always used to have very big engines but now, some of the best bikes have quite small ones, like Honda's CBR 600. This motorcycle is light, beautiful and quick. If you want to go any faster, you had better buy a jet plane!

Probably the best thing about bikes is that you can really get out and explore the world. Many riders think that the best motorcycles are the big trail bikes. These are the machines which were developed from the bikes which raced across the deserts for thousands of miles. They are big, powerful and tough. They have strong suspension which soaks up the bumps and large petrol tanks so that you can go for hundreds of miles without re-fuelling.

The first of the big trail bikes, and still one of the best, is the Yamaha Ténéré. The Ténéré is based on the bikes which raced in the Paris – Dacca rally, a 7,000 mile endurance race which goes through the North African desert. The Ténéré has a massive 25 litre petrol tank and a 750cc twin cylinder engine which will take the bike over the roughest country. Not many riders have raced their Ténérés in the desert, but instead, they use them for exploring the wild and lonely places of the world. Trail bikes can reach places only horses or people walking can go and because they are quiet, and do not damage the dirt roads, they are made welcome every-where.

Exploring on trail bikes has become

(Left) Trail riding gets you in places only bikes can reach.

(Below) The Honda Gold Wing is the ultimate luxury touring bike.

so popular that some companies, like Honda, even organise special holidays for riders of their bikes. One of the best biking trips in the world is the Transalp Rally in which riders of Honda's big trail bikes explore the parts of Europe tourists never normally see.

(Left) The Gold Wing "cockpit" is more like that of a plane than a bike.

Speedway

Speedway engine.

If you took all the things off a bike which were not really necessary to make it move you would be left with an engine, frame and two wheels – but not much of a real motorcycle. All motorcycles need brakes, suspension and gearboxes for them to be of any use. Well, **nearly** all bikes. There is one machine which has nothing but two wheels, a 500cc engine and a tiny frame which doesn't look strong enough for a pedal cycle. This is a speedway bike and seeing one of these machines in action is like nothing else in the world.

Speedway started in Australia over 60 years ago. The Australians liked going fast on their bikes and they found that they could race round the horse trotting tracks of the big country fairs which were held in New South Wales. The tracks were dirt covered so the bikes had to be slid round the corners, which is just how speedway riders turn today.

A few years later, speedway had come to Britain and thousands of people watched these daring young men slide their bikes round the oval dirt tracks, throwing up great clouds of dust. In 1930, most people had never even ridden a motorcycle or been in a car so the spectators could not believe their eyes when they saw the speedway riders throwing their bikes through the corners in great clouds of dust and cinders.

Everyone who watches

Speedway

Speedway bike.

a modern speedway meeting will still have the same feeling. How can anyone go so fast on a bike like that? It looks impossible. Let's look how the riders do those incredible things with their bikes.

A speedway machine has only those things which it really needs. There is not a single nut or bolt which is not essential. It doesn't need a gearbox, rear suspension, brakes or even a proper saddle so it doesn't have any.

But it does need a very powerful engine. There are four main makes of engine used in speedway racing. There are the British Godden and Weslake motors; the GM made in Italy and the Czechoslovakian Jawa. Although the four engines are from three different countries, they are all very similar in design. All the engines are four strokes which are built for racing and for nothing else. They are simple engines but are made from very good materials and this makes them expensive to buy and maintain. Instead of petrol, speedway engines burn methanol, which is refined wood alcohol. Methanol makes the engines run cooler and produces more power but these speedway engines use a gallon of methanol every six miles! Methanol wouldn't be any good for a road bike but speedway races are run over very short distances so the amount of fuel used doesn't matter so much.

A good speedway engine produces about 60 bhp. Because the whole bike only weighs about 75 kg and has such a powerful motor, the acceleration is fantastic. Giving a methanol burning engine full throttle is like letting a bomb off between your legs.

Ready for battle.

*Warming up the
bike.*

Speedway

The bikes are very low and light and are specially designed to slide. The track helps them to slide too. This is usually concrete with a thin layer of shale on top to make it slippery so that bike's wheels will slide easily.

There are usually four riders in a speedway race. They line up in front of a tape which shoots up when the starter begins the race. The riders let in their clutches instantly and because of their engines' power, the rear wheel spins. Each rider then moves back to make the wheel grip and tries to fight his way into the lead. Speedway riders are hard men and all four bikes will be nearly touching each other as they battle to get in front.

They enter the first corner at about 45 mph and lay their bikes over at the same time as leaning forward. The riders balance their bikes with their left leg. A rider's left foot has a special steel shoe covering the sole so that he can slide his foot on the ground without wearing it out.

Because the bikes are going nearly sideways, they lose a little bit of speed without needing any brakes. Then the riders give the engines full power and

Good starts are vital in speedway.

(Previous pages)
*Speedway is
all action!*

the rear wheel slides away letting the bike turn round the sharp corners. This sounds easy but it isn't – especially when there are three other riders determined to battle their way past you.

Speedway races are always four laps because the riders and bikes couldn't last any longer! A rider will have at least five races in a meeting and if he is a professional, he will ride four or five times a week. Riders score points for first, second and third places. Most races are between two teams and every rider's score counts.

There are individual races too for the World Championship. There have been some great British world champions, like Peter Craven and Peter Collins, but we are lucky in Britain because most world champions ride in the British League even if they were not born here. This is because the best, the hardest, speedway racing in the world is in Britain.

All speedway riders get paid for racing and many do nothing else. The top riders become very rich and are treated like pop stars. They have their own fan clubs and their leathers are covered with their sponsors' names.

The speedway season in Britain lasts from March until October and the top riders work hard for their money. As well as riding all over Britain in the evening speedway meetings, they will fly out to Germany at weekends for the important grass track races on a Sunday. Grass track is like speedway but on a grass field instead of a shale-covered track. For seven days a week they will do nothing but travel and race, earning as much money as possible before they get too old.

And in the British winter, what do they do for a change? Well, they go to Australia and ride in some more speedway!

Road Racing

Almost as soon as the first bikes were built, riders wanted to race them. It's not difficult to see why. Riding a motorcycle is always exciting but racing it against other riders is twice as much fun.

But bikes were not raced just for pleasure. Above all else, the early motorcycle manufacturers wanted to show that their bikes were reliable. No-one knows when the first bike race was held but we do know that in 1902, there was a competition from Paris to Vienna – a distance of about 800 miles (1300 km) and a long way to ride even

today. This race was won by a French Werner bike. The following year, bikes were timed at over 60 mph in a race at Nice, in the south of France. They went nearly twice as fast as the quickest horse, which was about the fastest thing to race before bikes.

The Isle of Man TT races soon became the most important road races in the world. The first race was held in 1907 but as bikes became better, they were moved to a long, $37\frac{3}{4}$ mile (60 km) circuit which twists and turns from one end of the Isle of Man to the other. It is on this difficult, dangerous

A British Manx Norton – the best road racing machine of the 1950s.

track that some of the greatest road races in the world have been seen.

For many people, the best ever road racer was Mike Hailwood. He was a very quiet, modest man who began his career riding British AJS and Norton bikes. In a few years, he had come from nothing to be a TT star! Then, in 1965, the 500 cc Senior TT race was held in a gale force storm. The rain was so bad that the spectators could hardly see the course and the riders were blinded by the wind and spray. Mike was riding an Italian MV Agusta bike and crashed. Everyone thought he was finished but he kicked the damaged bike straight and rode on to win. Lots of fans think that

this is the greatest race ever seen on the TT circuit.

There have been many fabulous racing bikes too but the most successful of all is Honda. Many star riders rode Honda in the Isle of Man races, including Mike Hailwood, and by 1987, Honda had won every class for solo bikes – a really incredible achievement.

The TT circuit is still used today but not for the main World Championship races. Many riders think that the long circuit, surrounded by stone walls and hedges, is too dangerous for the very fast modern bikes. Now, the Grand Prix races are held on special circuits which have wide, safe corners and

The world's best ever road racer in one of his greatest races. Mike Hailwood aboard his badly damaged 500cc MV Agusta in the 1965 Isle of Man TT. Despite the terrible weather and all the problems he faced, Mike went on to win. (Photo: Don Morley)

Road Racing

special run-off areas at the edge of the track which slow a rider down if he crashes.

There are four solo classes in Grand Prix road racing and a special category for sidecars. The solos are the 80cc; 125cc; 250cc and 500cc. Each class is exciting in its own way. On the little bikes, the riders lay almost glued to their bikes. They have to keep every part of their body hidden behind the fairing and windscreen so that the wind does not slow them down by even the tiniest amount.

On the 500 cc bikes, there is almost too much power! A bike like Wayne Gardner's Grand Prix Honda will produce over 140 bhp. If Wayne is careless when he uses the throttle, the Honda will stand up on its back wheel in a giant wheelie. Or it might slide from underneath him like a speedway bike. Sometimes, it will do both things together! 500 cc Grand Prix racing is the most spectacular kind of road racing.

Manufacturers are still testing new parts on their road racing bikes, just

Martinez stows himself well away on his 80cc Derbi to win a World title.
(Photo: Don Morley)

(Above and opposite page) Many safety features found on modern bikes have come from road racing machines like the powerful disc brakes and huge back tyres.

like they did 80 years ago, to see if they will be suitable for road bikes. If you look at a Grand Prix road racer, you will see huge disc brakes on the front and rear wheels. A 500 cc road racing bike can easily travel at 180 mph and you need good brakes to stop! The front suspension will have an anti-dive device on the front forks. This stops the front of the bike dropping when the brakes are used hard and also helps to prevent skids. Now, many road bikes have discs on the front and rear wheels and they also have anti-dive fitted to front forks as well.

Road racing engines produce tremendous power. If you can imagine something which will do from 0–100 mph quicker than you can read this paragraph, then that's how fast a modern road racer goes!

All Grand Prix bikes have two-stroke engines because these produce the most power and are the lightest. The 500 cc bikes have four cylinders and disc-valves. They all have six-speed gearboxes and extremely strong clutches. Although they are so powerful, they are useless for anything except road racing. After every single event, they have to be completely stripped down and checked, and all the worn parts must be replaced. All this is very expensive and the top teams, like Honda, spend millions of pounds on racing every year.

Working with the race teams are the sponsors. Companies like Castrol help to pay for the cost of running the factory teams and like the bike makers, they use racing to improve their products. Many of Castrol's oils were designed using information gained whilst they were racing. Dunlop do the same job with their tyres. Everyone

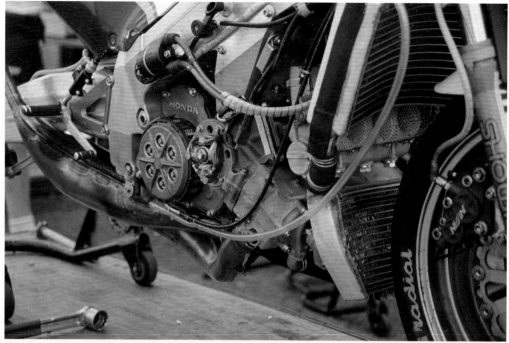

The incredibly powerful 4 cylinder Honda Grand Prix road racing engine.

A huge team is needed to support a Grand Prix road racer.

learns a lot about making motor-cycling safer from their racing experience.

There is one Grand Prix class which is very different from all the others and that is the sidecar. The British team of Steve Webster and Tony Hewitt were the World Champions in 1987, 1988 and 1989. In sidecar racing, the passenger and driver must work as a close team. They have to rely on each other completely and unless the passenger balances the sidecar perfectly on corners, the outfit will crash. Some of the best passengers are girls. Because they are quick and brave, they can move around the outfit at exactly the right time so the driver can go as quick as possible.

Many solo riders think that the side-car people are just a little bit crazy but they are certainly fast and spec-tacular!

Wayne Gardner at the British Grand Prix.
(Photo: Don Morley)

Motocross

(Opposite page)
Bikes can fly!
Hakan Carlqvist –
500 Kawasaki.

All bike racing is spectacular but the best of all is motocross. It's the toughest, and most exciting kind of racing ever.

Motorcyclists have always treated their bikes as if they were alive. The rider sits on a bike like he would sit on a horse and the wind blows in his face, just as if he were galloping along. But most of all, a bike behaves as if it is a fine horse. It will gallop and jump and climb up the side of hills you would find hard to walk up on foot. Nothing else with an engine behaves like this.

When the early motorcyclists found out that they had "iron horses" instead of just machines, they wanted to see just what these fantastic new animals could do. So they raced them across the roughest tracks and through the deepest streams and in the muddiest bogs. They called this new sport, "scrambling" because the riders had to scramble about to keep on their bikes.

Gradually, the "scrambles" became races with rules and when the riders from Europe took up the sport, they changed its name to motocross – which comes from the English word "cross" and part of the French word for bike, which is "moto". So a race across country on a bike became a motocross. Although the modern bikes and riders are very different, motocross is still the toughest and most exciting kind of motor sport.

In motocross, the riders race around a specially designed course. The track will have big jumps which the riders leap over and very rough, bumpy sections which throw the bike all over the track. There will be sharp corners which the racers slide their bikes round at a few miles an hour and fast straights where they will go at nearly road racing speeds. All the time, the

Dave Thorpe and Sharon.

(Opposite page) Dave Thorpe's 500cc Grand Prix Honda – like riding a runaway rocket.

Motocross can be fast!

motocross bikes are twisting and turning and shaking like live animals and the riders have to concentrate very hard if they want to stay on.

As well as beating the track, there are the other riders. Motocross racers are really tough and they will do anything to pass the person in front. So just as you are leaping through the air over a big jump, you can easily find someone flying over your head as he passes you. That's why motocross is the most exciting sport in the world!

To ride motocross you have to be fit – very fit indeed. Most motocross riders train in the gym. They will lift weights and go out running so that they are strong enough to ride their bikes. Motocross riders are the fittest of all motorcycle racers.

Even though it is so exciting, motocross is quite safe and very few riders are ever really badly injured. One of the reasons for the safety is that the racers wear such good equipment. Everyone has to wear racing helmets and many of these have ventilation systems to try to keep the rider

A typical motocross bike. Note the huge spaces between the mudguards and tyres to allow for the long wheel travel as the suspension soaks up the bumps on the track.

cool as he fights the bike over the bumps and jumps. He will also wear body armour so that he doesn't get cut by the stones which are thrown up by the bikes in front. To protect his feet, the rider wears strong boots with stiff plastic fronts and flat soles which slide over the rough ground when the rider puts his foot down to steady the bike.

Throughout the race, the rider always wears goggles so that his eyes are not injured by the flying stones and dust. Covering the lens of the goggles, are four or five strips of thin plastic which he can throw away during the race as they get covered in mud. These are called tear-offs.

Motocross machines are just as special as motocross riders. They have the best suspension of any kind of bike. The front forks have about 300 mm of travel and the rear even more.

This lets each wheel absorb tremendous shocks without breaking or throwing the rider off the bike. Imagine jumping off the top of a van travelling down the motorway at 60 mph. That's what it's like landing a motocross bike after a fast jump.

The frames on motocross bikes are very light but they are also extremely strong. There is nothing on the bike which is not for racing. There are no lights, speedometer or even a stand. Everything which is not essential for motocross is left off to save weight.

Most motocross engines are single cylinder two-strokes but they are nothing like the two-stroke moped engines we looked at earlier in the book. These engines bite! The instant the rider opens the throttle, he has tremendous power available so that the steepest hills can be climbed as if they were not there or the deepest mud blasted through like a puddle on the pavement. Just opening the throttle will make the bike wheelie and if the rider is not very careful, he will be thrown off the back! There are many good girl riders and motocross is a sport where men and women compete together on equal terms. At the moment, the men are the best because they are bigger and stronger but women are getting better all the time.

Children compete too in youth races. The youngest who can race are just seven years old but this is not sensible. The best age to begin racing is about 14 when the young person's body is fit and strong enough to take the bumps and knocks of motocross without suffering any damage.

One of the best motocross riders in the world is Dave Thorpe, who lives in the south of England near Heathrow airport. He has been World Champion three times in the 500 cc class – which is the one where all the best riders compete. Dave is a very quiet man who doesn't look a bit like a racer when you see him in a business suit but on the track, he is a tough rider. Although all the Japanese companies and several European manufacturers produce motocross machines most of

Signalling is vital to the front runners so that they know exactly where they are in a race.

the big races are won by Honda bikes because they are so good.

Dave is a professional rider – he races motocross for a job – and is very rich indeed. But he works very hard, training in gym and running and then spending hours practising and trying to improve the bikes and his riding.

During the motocross season, Dave travels over 40,000 miles all over the world. The motocross season begins in March and carries on until August with races in most of the European countries and America too. It's a tough way to earn a living but an exciting one too. Because he is such a good sportsman as well as a brilliant rider, Dave has made everyone in Britain proud of him. Perhaps you might follow in his footsteps one day and take part in the most exciting sport in the world, for motocross is truly THE sport.

What Do They Mean?

Aluminium Foil – A good way of making a motorcycle jacket warm. A very thin layer of aluminium-coated plastic is put between the inside and outside of the jacket and reflects the heat from the rider's body and so keeps him warm.

Battery – All bikes have a battery. This provides electricity for the lights when the engine is only running slowly and for the ignition when the bike is started. It will also turn the starter motor if the bike has an electric starter. The battery must be well charged with electricity or it won't work. Many of a bike's electrical problems come from a battery which isn't working properly. The battery is charged by the **generator**. This must work well if the battery is to be fully charged. If you have problems with the generator, you can't mend it at home.

Belt Drive – The leather belt the veteran bikes used to drive their rear wheel before chains became reliable. They are terrible in wet conditions when they slip and won't work. A new kind of toothed belt is used on a few bikes, like Harley-Davidson, because it is cleaner and quieter than a chain but not as strong.

Big Four Japanese Motorcycle Makers – Nearly all the bikes in the world are made by four Japanese factories: Honda, Yamaha, Suzuki and Kawasaki. Honda is the biggest and most important. The four Japanese factories make every kind of bike you can imagine and all of them work well. The Japanese became the most important motorcycle makers by producing better bikes for every purpose than the Europeans.

BMW – A German maker of bikes and cars. The company produces high quality, and very expensive, motorcycles. Some of the best sports touring machines in the world are made by BMW.

British Motorcycle Industry – Once Britain had the biggest motorcycle industry in the world with firms like BSA, Triumph, Norton and Matchless making every kind of bike from Grand Prix road racers to commuter bikes. In the 1960s, one firm after another collapsed because the bikes they were making were not as good as the Japanese machines. Now, there is Norton making a small number of high quality bikes and a few tiny companies producing frames with European engines. Triumph now has a new generation of bikes on sale so perhaps there might be a British motorcycle industry once again.

Brooklands – The famous race track in Surrey used by cars and bikes before the war. Really a hugh concrete saucer around which the bikes could go absolutely flat out. In the 1930s, every motorcyclist wanted a Brooklands' Gold Star which was given for a 100 mph lap, during a race.

BSI – The British Standards Institution. This is an organization which sets

75

safety standards for everything from toasters to electric plugs. It tests thousands of different designs each year to make sure that they are safe and work well. BSI sets the standards for helmets, goggles and visors which motorcyclists use. We are very lucky to have the BSI in Britain.

Clutch – This is part of the gearbox and lets the rider disconnect the engine for a moment so that the gears can be changed. When it is let in slowly, it lets the rider pull away from a standstill. The clutch lever is on the left-hand side of the handlebar.

Craftsmen – The very skilled workers who used to make bikes by hand. Now, computer-controlled machines have replaced craftsmen but in the 1930s, British metal workers were the best in the world and made motorcycles which are still beautiful to look at and ride, even now.

Crankshaft – The shaft which goes through the centre of the engine. When the piston is pushed down by the petrol exploding in the engine, the crankshaft is turned by the **connecting rod**. Imagine you were on a pedal cycle and your body was the engine. You make your legs push down just as if they were the connecting rod. Your legs then move the pedals which are like a motorcycle's crankshaft. As the crankshaft turns, it can spin the gearbox which then drives the back wheel.

Credit Facilities – Most dealers will be able to arrange for you to borrow money to buy a bike but you don't **have** to borrow the money through them. The banks will also lend you money. What you are looking for is the lowest possible **APR** (annual percentage rate). The lower the APR number then the less the loan will cost you. Also, the shorter the period of time you borrow the money, then the less it will cost you. **All** loans are expensive. The best way to buy a bike is to save the money first, before you buy anything.

Economical – This means that something doesn't cost a lot to run. Commuter bikes, like Honda's CM90, are economical. You can travel to work every day and use very little petrol. All commuter bikes are very economical to run.

Enduros – Bike racers say that enduro riders are the most intelligent motorcyclists. In an enduro, a rider has to race over all sorts of ground from deep bogs to fast shale roads and this all has to be done without any practise. Instead, the enduro racer just follows brightly coloured arrows trying to keep to a speed schedule the organizers have set. Enduro riders have to be as skilful as trials riders; as fit as a motocrosser and as brave as a road racer. Enduros are really good fun to ride.

Engineers – The men who design the bikes.

Frame – This is the structure which holds the engine, the front suspension and the rear suspension. A bike frame is usually made from steel tubing and must be very strong so that it doesn't twist or flex. If it does, then the bike will handle badly and could be dangerous.

Gearbox – The part of the engine which contains the gears. This is always behind the engine and before the swinging-arm. Most modern bikes have five or six gears, controlled by a lever on the left-hand side of the engine. Pressing it down will make the gearbox change to lower gears for starting off and climbing hills and lifting it up changes to higher gears for cruising at faster speeds.

Grass Track Racing – Like speedway but on a flat grass field. There are a lot of grass tracks in Britain and they are great to ride in and good to watch.

Great Depression – The time in the 1930s when there was very high unemployment and many of the British and European motorcycle makers struggled to keep going.

Mike Hailwood – Still the greatest road racer who has ever lived. He could ride any sort of motorcycle brilliantly and no matter how bad the bike was, he could make it win. He was most famous for his rides on the Italian MV Agusta bikes and later, Hondas. Sadly he was killed by a lorry whilst he was driving a car.

Harley-Davidson – The last major American manufacturer of bikes. The company is famous for its V twin motors, which are used in the best choppers, and also some fantastic street bikes.

Headlamp – The large light on the front of the bike.

Highway Code – The rules which all road users have to know and understand. The Highway Code not only tells you about the laws which you have to obey when you are riding but also gives a lot of good, sensible advice on safe riding. You will be asked questions on the Highway Code when you take your full driving test.

Hobby – Something somebody does for fun. Many bikes now are used for a hobby instead of just a way for getting about.

Instructor – The person who will teach you how to ride a bike. All instructors are excellent riders and make learning to ride a bike as much fun as possible. A motorcycle school will provide the most enjoyable lessons you have ever had!

Insurance – It is illegal – and very stupid – to ride a bike without insurance. It is also illegal to let one of your friends ride your bike. Your dealer will be able to sell you motorcycle insurance but you can also go to an **Insurance Broker** who might be able to get you cheaper insurance. There is more than one company selling

77

motorcycle insurance and they do not all charge the same.

Iron Horse – Motorcycles are very special machines and behave almost like animals. Motorcyclists soon came to love their bikes like horse riders loved their animals. A good rider can make a bike do anything he wants just as if the bike were alive. That's why riders call their bikes **"Iron Horses"**.

Isle of Man TT Races – The famous races held round the $37\frac{3}{4}$ mile course in the Isle of Man in June. The course is on ordinary public roads and is very dangerous if the rider makes a mistake but some of best road races ever seen have taken place there. Many riders think that the TT course is too dangerous for modern bikes.

Learner Rider – A rider who is just beginning to learn motorcycling. You will need a bike, insurance, a helmet and training before you can go on the road as a learner rider.

Leathers – The leather suit or jacket which every biker really wants to own. They give excellent protection but make sure you only buy cow-hide or goat-skin. Great for posing in too!

Maintenance – Looking after your bike so that it will run well. Bikes are fun to work on and even a beginner can do most of the basic maintenance at home.

Merchantable Quality – The legal term for something doing the job it is sold for. If you buy a bike from a dealer, it will have to be of **"Merchantable Quality"**. This means that the bike will work properly and be safe to ride. If you buy a bike from an ordinary person, it can be in any condition. For this reason, it is a good idea to buy your first bike from a dealer.

Moped – A 50 cc bike with a restricted engine which means that you can't travel much more than 30 mph. Not much fun – but just about better than pedalling.

MoT Certificate – All bikes over three years old have to be examined by a specially-trained mechanic to see that they are safe to ride on the road. It is illegal to ride a bike without an MoT certificate and silly too, because the MoT test is a very useful safety check. Before you buy a bike, either from a dealer or private individual, make sure that the machine has just had an MoT test and ask to see the certificate.

Motocross – The most exciting of all the motorcycle sports. Riders race over rough ground, jumping and sliding their bikes about. Motocross is the toughest bike sport of all and you have to be very fit and very brave to do well at it.

Noise – All noisy motorcycles are bad. Bikes can be fun without being noisy and there is no reason at all for having a noisy motorcycle. The fastest Super Bikes in the world are also the quietest. Altering the bike's exhaust can damage the engine and will make it go slower. Only idiots ride noisy bikes.

Norton – Until Triumph launched their new range of three and four cylinder four-stroke super-bikes, Norton was the only real manufacturer of motorcycles in Britain. Norton bikes use a Wankel rotary engine which is very smooth, quiet and fast. The Nortons are beautifully made bikes but are expensive and made only for a few enthusiasts.

Piston – The part of the engine which moves up and down inside the **cylinder** barrel, pushed down by the burning gases. Imagine a tube with a can inside sliding up and down. The cylinder barrel will be like the tube and the can like the piston.

Rallying – Events where riders meet each other, sometimes from all over the world. There are prizes for the furthest travelled rider; the best looking bike and the most interesting one. Touring riders go to rallies to meet other tourers. Rallies are very relaxed and easy going.

Road Racing – The fastest of all the motorcycle sports where riders race against each other on tarmac tracks. There is a road race held somewhere in Britain on every weekend throughout the summer.

Seams – The joint on riding jackets and over-trousers. Seams should always be strong and either welded – joined together without any stitching – or have a waterproof tape underneath the stitching. On a good jacket, the seams will always be waterproof.

Second-hand – When a bike has been owned by someone else and is not new. Most riders begin with a second-hand bike which is cheaper than a new one. Providing a second-hand bike is in good condition, it can be just as good as a new one.

Spark Plug – This is in the top of the engine and when it sparks, it ignites the mixture of petrol and air which is fed into the engine by the **carburettor**. This mixture explodes and pushes the piston down very quickly.

Sports Bike – Usually means a very fast road bike which often looks like a road racer.

Super Bike – The super sports bike. The first **Super Bike** was the **Z1 Kawasaki** which was the fastest bike of its day. Now, all Super Bikes will reach 150 mph easily: great fun but only for experienced riders.

Thinsulate – A very thin, warm padding which goes inside motorcycle clothing and makes it comfortable to wear, even in cold weather.

Dave Thorpe – The British motocross rider. A fine athlete; a good sportsman and three times World 500cc motocross champion.

Throttle – The movable grip on the right-hand side of the bike which makes the bike go faster or slower as you turn it.

Trials – A difficult kind of motorcycle sport where riders have to go over extremely rough ground without stopping or putting their feet down. The best trials riders are incredible and can ride their special trials bikes up waterfalls or over huge rocks without any difficulty. Although the speeds are only slow, trials riding needs a lot of skill.

Triumph – One of the most famous, and most successful British bike makers. Now producing an exciting range of three and four cylinder superbikes which look as if they will be as good as anything made in Japan. Triumph say that they will make 10,000 bikes a year which will mean that they will be one of the biggest non-Japanese manufacturers.

Veteran Bikes – The oldest bikes made before 1915. There are still a lot of these bikes kept running by owners who love them dearly. Interesting to see if you ever get the chance.

Vintage Bikes – Motorcycles made in the period 1915 until the end of 1930. Some of the very best British bikes were made at this time. Tremendous fun to ride but expensive to buy now.

Visor – The clear polycarbonate shield which covers the front of a full face helmet. Always ride with your visor down because your eyes are easily damaged. Modern visors are very safe and give tremendous protection.

Workshop Manual – A book full of practical advice which will enable you to maintain and repair your bike. Haynes, the publisher of this book, also publish a huge range of "Owners Workshop Manuals" for motorcycles.